Days at the Beach

words by Amanda Graham
photographs by Russell Millard

Sunday

Grandma and I went to the beach.

I found lots of things.

Monday

I found a shell.

Once an animal lived in it.

Tuesday

I found some seaweed.

Once it was on the sea bed.

Wednesday

I found a dead crab.

Once it lived in a rock pool.

Thursday

I found some wood.

Once it was part of a tree.

Friday

I found a feather.

Once it was on a bird.

Saturday

I found some footprints.

Once someone was there.

It was my grandma.